A first guide to

◆

Russia

By Kath Davies

A ZOË BOOK

© 1995 Zoë Books Limited

Devised and produced by
Zoë Books Limited
15 Worthy Lane
Winchester
Hampshire SO23 7AB
England

Illustrative material used in this book first appeared in *Discovering Russia*, published by Zoe Books Limited.

First published in Great Britain in 1995 by
Zoë Books Limited
15 Worthy Lane
Winchester
Hampshire SO23 7AB

A record of the CIP data is available from the British Library.

ISBN 1 874488 37 1

Printed in Italy by Grafedit SpA
Design: Jan Sterling, Sterling Associates
Editor: Denise Allard
Picture research: Victoria Sturgess
Map: Gecko Limited
Production: Grahame Griffiths

Photographic acknowledgments

The publishers wish to acknowledge, with thanks, the following photographic sources:

Cover and title page: The Hutchison Library; 5 The Hutchison Library / Vladimir Bireus; 6 Tony Stone Images; 7l & r Robert Harding Picture Library; 8 Bruce Coleman Ltd / Hans Reinhard; 9l Robert Harding Picture Library; 9r, 10 Zefa; 11l Bruce Coleman Ltd / Steve Kaufman; 11r, 12 Magnum Photos/Fred Mayer; 13l The Hutchison Library / Victoria Juleva; 13r Impact Photos / Bradshaw; 14 Zefa; 15l Magnum Photos/Peter Marlow; 15r Robert Harding Picture Library; 16 Zefa; 17l Robert Harding Picture Library; 17r Zefa; 18 The Hutchison Library / Igor Gavrilov; 19l Zefa; 19r The Hutchison Library / Victoria Juleva; 20 Robert Harding Picture Library; 21l Magnum Photos / Abbas; 21r The Hutchison Library / John Egan; 22 Sporting Pictures; 23l The Wernher Collection, Luton Hoo; 23r Zefa; 24 Robert Harding Picture Library; 25 The Kobal Collection; 26, 27l & r Mary Evans Picture Library; 28 Mary Evans / Alexander Meledin Collection; 29l Peter Newark's Military Pictures; 29r DDA Photo Library

Cover: *Outside the Kremlin, in Moscow*

Title page: *A boy sitting on the steps of his old Russian house*

Contents

Russian words are shown in *italics* and are explained in the text.

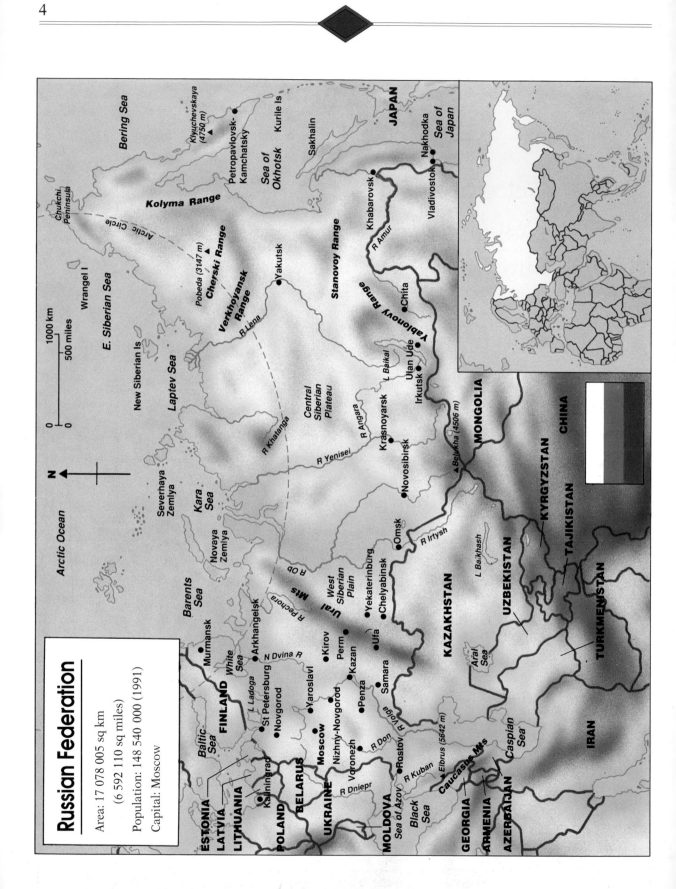

Russian Federation

Area: 17 078 005 sq km
(6 592 110 sq miles)

Population: 148 540 000 (1991)

Capital: Moscow

Welcome to Russia!

A group of lands make up the area which is usually called 'Russia'. The proper name for this group is the Russian Federation. Russia is one of 11 countries which make up the Commonwealth of Independent States (CIS).

Russia is the largest country in the world. It is nearly twice the size of the United States of America, and is 70 times bigger than Britain. As the sun sets in western Russia, it is rising in the far east of the country.

More than 148 million people live in Russia, but they are not all Russians. The country is also home to Cossacks, Bashkirs and the Tartar peoples. Some of these peoples speak Russian, others have their own language and customs.

Russian, like Polish and Czech, is part of the Slav group of languages. There are about 25 million Russians who live outside Russia. They speak Russian as well as the language of the countries where they live. The Russian alphabet is more than 1100 years old. The Russian word for 'Welcome' is *Privetstviye*.

▼ Visitors in Moscow's Red Square

West of the Urals

The city of St Petersburg is built on about 100 islands at the mouth of the River Neva. From here, ships sail to ports in the Baltic Sea and the North Sea.

St Petersburg is very beautiful. It was the capital city of Russia between 1713 and 1918. It has many fine buildings, bridges and fountains. The Winter Palace and the Hermitage are famous for their collections of paintings.

Kaliningrad is another western seaport. It is a base for the Russian navy, and for trade.

▼ St Petersburg from the River Neva

What's in a name?

Sometimes cities and streets have changed their names. St Petersburg was once called Petrograd ('Peter's city'). It then became Leningrad, after a famous leader called Lenin. Now it is St Petersburg again.

Cities of the west

Most people live in the western part of Russia. There are many big industrial cities here. In Samara and Nizhny-Novgorod they make cars, aircraft and trains. At Rostov, on the River Don, there are shipbuilding yards. People in Rostov also work in textile mills and in factories where they make chemicals.

▼ The snowy peak of Mount Elbrus

▲ The Volga is Europe's longest river

European Russia

The Ural Mountains form Europe's border with Asia. West of the Urals, there is a great plain. Forests of pine and birch trees grow there. The plain is warm in summer, but winters are very cold.

The River Volga flows across the plain. It is 3690 kilometres (2293 miles) from its source to the Caspian Sea. It is the longest river in Europe.

Elbrus is the highest peak in Europe. It is in the Caucasus Mountains, and is 5642 metres (18 511 feet) high.

Into Siberia

It takes eight days to travel by train from Moscow through Siberia to the east coast!

Siberia means 'the sleeping land'. The Siberian Plain is a huge area of flat land, with marshes and great rivers such as the Ob. It stretches from the frozen Arctic in the north to the hot sandy deserts of Kazakhstan. The endless forests, called the *taiga*, lie in between.

Winter snows last from September to May, but the short, hot summers bring flowers. Wolves and brown bears live in Siberia.

▼ Two young brown bears playing in the snow

▲ The Trans-Siberian Railway

At the centre of Russia

The famous Trans-Siberian Railway was built in 1905. It runs for 9438 kilometres (5865 miles) from Moscow to Nakhodka on the Sea of Japan. Trains stop at 90 stations on the way! Modern branch lines go to Mongolia and to China.

The railway passes villages of small wooden houses. It also links towns and cities, where there are blocks of flats and factories with tall chimneys.

Siberia's largest cities are in the south, near Russia's border with Kazakhstan. Although most of Siberia is empty wilderness, it is rich in natural resources, such as oil and gas.

The rocks contain iron ore, gold and diamonds, and there are millions of trees for timber.

Lake Baikal is near the town of Irkutsk. It is called the 'Pearl of Siberia' because it is so beautiful. About 336 rivers flow into this lake, and only one flows out. Baikal is the deepest lake in the world, at 1940 metres (6365 feet). More than 50 different kinds of fish live in the lake. In winter, people catch the fish through holes in the ice!

▼ On the shores of Lake Baikal

Arctic Russia

Northern Russia is a land of ice, which borders the Arctic Ocean. The seaports are Murmansk and Arkhangelsk. Ships called ice-breakers keep the harbour open at Arkhangelsk. About half a million people live in each of these cities.

▲ Stuck in the ice until spring

▲ Reindeer herds feed on moss

Beyond the White Sea, there are lonely islands where wildlife such as polar bears, seals and walrus live. The frozen sea never melts at the North Pole.

Across the tundra

Snow covers Arctic Russia for most of the year. The land stays frozen all the time, even when the snow melts. Trees cannot grow here, but there are mosses and small shrubs. Land like this is called tundra.

On rivers such as the Lena, the ice is so thick in winter that trucks and cars use it as a road. In summer, barges travel on water from the melted ice.

Herders and hunters

People earn their living by herding reindeer, hunting and fishing. They used to wander with their herds, but today most people live in villages. They use rifles to hunt wildfowl.

The Lapp people live on the border with Norway, and the Komi and the Nentsi peoples live in the northwest.

▼ A hunter skis cross-country

Travelling east

Eastern Siberia is another very cold region. Only about a million people live here, in a land the size of India. The towns here may be 800 kilometres (500 miles) apart. Sometimes it is too cold for the children to go to school. They have lessons on television.

▼ In Yakutsk, milk is frozen in blocks!

▲ Life on the island of Sakhalin

The Russian Far East has natural resources such as oil, coal and other minerals underground. There are forests for timber, and fish around the coasts.

Beyond the River Lena, high mountains stretch to the north and the south. The River Amur marks the border between the Russian Federation and China. There are 30 active volcanoes on the Kamchatka peninsula and on the island of Sakhalin.

In the next 20 years, a new city may be built in the east, near Vladivostok. There will be a harbour and a canal, and new road, rail and air links to other cities.

Pacific Russia

From the Russian island of Ratmanov you can see across to the mountains of Alaska, in the USA. Alaska once belonged to Russia, but was sold to the Americans in 1867.

Russia has quarrelled with Japan and with China about their borders. There is still an argument about who owns some of the Kurile Islands.

Vladivostok

The biggest city on the Pacific coast of Russia is Vladivostok. It is a port on the Sea of Japan, and is a base for the Russian navy. About 600 000 people live in the city.

▼ The lights of Vladivostok

MOSCOW

The Russian Federation is ruled, or governed, from the city of Moscow. Moscow lies at the heart of European Russia. We know that it was there nearly 850 years ago, because a prince called Yuri gave a great feast there. Long ago, there were monasteries around Moscow.
Now there are rings of motorways and railways around the city. At the centre of Moscow lies the Kremlin.

Kremlin is a Russian word for 'fort'. The Moscow Kremlin has red walls. Inside the walls there are palaces, offices, museums and parks. The cathedral has golden domes. The rulers of Russia used to meet in the Kremlin. Today, the Russian Parliament meets in the White House. It is a modern building near the river.

▼ The Kremlin, beside the Moscow River

The Kremlin walls contain the tombs of many famous Russians. Outside the walls are streets of shops, parks, houses, factories and blocks of flats.

Travelling around

Moscow has an underground railway called the Metro. Its stations are very grand, with statues and chandeliers. The trains carry five million passengers every day!

Moscow has good road, rail and air links. There are also river and canal links to the coast. Barges carry goods such as grain and timber by water.

▲ St Basil's Cathedral, Red Square

Out and about in Moscow

St Basil's Cathedral has coloured domes and spires. It is almost 440 years old. It looks over Moscow's famous Red Square, where many parades are held.

One smart shopping area is called GUM. The letters stand for State Universal Store. About 350 000 people visit the new shops and cafés in GUM every day. Other people like to shop at the street stalls.

▼ Winter in Moscow

Russia at work

In 1917, the Bolshevik, or Communist, Party came to power. They wanted to make life better for the working people of Russia.

The new government believed that the people, or state, should own everything. They changed the way in which farms and factories were run, and they built new factories. The country was now called the Soviet Union. Many of the changes were good, but some changes brought hardship and hunger. Some of the new leaders imprisoned or killed people who disagreed with them.

Since 1991, Russia has been governed in a different way. Business people from other countries may now work in Russia.

▼ A statue shows a factory worker and a farmer

▲ Herding cattle

However, not all Russians feel that their lives are better now. There are not enough jobs, and shops often run out of goods to sell.

Russia's riches

Russia has a great deal of coal, oil and natural gas. The Ural Mountains contain copper, iron ore, gold and diamonds in their rocks. There is timber from the forests, and fish from the seas.

Cattle are raised in Siberia and in western Russia. On the southern steppes, farmers grow wheat, barley and maize.

Power and pollution

Pollution is a problem in some areas. The waste from factories spoils the water in the rivers, the air and the land, and harms people who live nearby.

There have been more than 200 accidents at nuclear power stations since 1992.

In space

The Soviet Union became a world leader in exploring space. It was the first to send women and men into space. Now scientists have used space mirrors to reflect sunlight on to Earth. One day, they may warm up Siberia!

▼ Piles of timber, Novosibirsk

Daily life

The communist government tried to look after the people. It provided free education and healthcare. Everyone had a place to live and a job. The government had to borrow money from other countries to pay for these benefits.

▲ Shopping can take a long time!

Today, the new government no longer controls prices. People pay more rent for their homes, and goods cost more because shopkeepers can fix their own prices. Russians have more freedom, but there are new problems.

▲ An old Russian country house

Housing and homes

In Russian cities, most people live in small flats. Families may have to share a kitchen and a bathroom. In many families, grandparents and parents live together. Sometimes people buy or build a block of flats together. This is called a co-operative. Each family pays part of the cost.

In the countryside, people usually live in houses. Some of the houses are made of wood. They look pretty, but they may not have electricity or water!

Many Russian people are returning to Russia from other countries. They all need homes. There are also many Russian soldiers who were stationed abroad and who are now in Russia. They too need houses. Some of these people have to live in tents because there are not yet enough houses or flats for them.

▼ In a kitchen in St Petersburg

Food and drink

Some dishes are favourites all over Russia. Beetroot soup is very popular. It is called *borshch*. Another favourite dish is made with thin strips of beef. The beef is cooked with mushrooms, onion, black pepper and sour cream. Its name is beef *stroganov*. Everyone loves small pancakes called *blinis*.

▼ Melons, fruit and salads for a feast

▲ Tea from a *samovar*

There are many recipes for cooking the fish which come from Russia's lakes and rivers. The most famous Russian fish dish is made from fish eggs, or roe. This is called caviar. Special black caviar comes from the huge Beluga sturgeon. This fish lives in the Caspian Sea and can be four metres (13 feet) long. Red caviar is salmon roe.

Russian drinks

Russian tea is made using a large urn called a *samovar*. Russians drink tea without milk. They add jam or sugar to sweeten it.

Russians also like to drink vodka. It is made from wheat, grain or potatoes, and is very strong. People also enjoy beer, wine, and a drink made from bread and honey, called *kvas*.

Eating out

For many years, only rich people could eat out. Now there are cafés, and food stalls which sell coffee or hot meat snacks, such as *shashlik*.

▼ Shopping for food in Moscow

Sports and the arts

Russian people enjoy sports. Their teams have won many medals at the Olympic Games. Skating, swimming and gymnastics are very popular. In winter there are ice hockey matches, and in summer people watch football games. They play chess and go boating in the parks. There are hot steam rooms and cool pools to relax in at the public baths.

Schools close for three months holiday in the summer. Children go to summer camp or stay in the country with their grandparents.

▲ Champion gymnast, Sergei Charkov, 1993

▲ Picture frames made by the court jeweller, Fabergé

Many families have a small country house, or *dacha*. They may grow vegetables there.

At New Year, Grandfather Frost brings presents for the children. Christmas Day is 7 January.

Paintings and fine arts

Some of the oldest Russian religious paintings are called *icons*. They were once hung in every home and in churches. Russian jewellers were famous all over the world. Artists at one time painted mostly heroes and heroines but, today, artists paint in many different styles.

Poets and writers

Many well-known writers are Russian. These include Leo Tolstoy (1828-1910), a novel writer, and Anton Chekhov (1860-1904) who wrote plays.

In the spotlight

People enjoy going to the opera, the theatre and the ballet. Music concerts are also very popular. Folk songs are sung to a string instrument, or *balalaika*.

Two famous ballet companies are the Bolshoi in Moscow and the Kirov in St Petersburg. The composer Peter Tchaikovsky (1840-1893) wrote music for some of the best loved ballets.

▼ The Kirov Ballet in *Swan Lake*

Russia in history

The first people who lived in the Russian lands were Stone Age hunters. They moved across Asia towards the Baltic Sea. About 2500 years ago, people called Scythians lived in the southern plains. They rode horses, and were famous for their skill at archery. About 1000 years ago, Vikings from Scandinavia sailed down the rivers of Russia. At first they attacked villages and took slaves, but later they traded goods with the people.

▲ The monastery at Sergiev was founded in 1337

The country in the northwest was called Rus, and the first Russian state capital was the town of Kiev. It was a trading centre for furs which came from beyond the Urals.

About 1000 years ago, travellers from Greece and Turkey brought Christianity to Russia. Two hundred years later, the Tartars attacked from the east, and Sweden and Germany attacked from the north and the west. The hero Prince Alexander Nevsky defeated both armies.

▼ From *Alexander Nevsky*, a film by Eisenstein

The first *tsars*

Grand Prince Ivan III, or 'Ivan the Great', ruled from 1462-1505. He was the first Russian leader to call himself the emperor, or *tsar*. Ivan's symbol was a two-headed eagle.

Ivan's grandson was called Ivan 'the Terrible', because he was so cruel. He conquered the Tartar lands in the east.

In 1598 a nobleman called Boris Godunov became *tsar*. After he died, Sweden invaded the north, and Poland held the city of Moscow.

A great empire

Tsar Peter I ruled from 1682 until 1725. During his long reign, he brought many changes to Russia. Peter was interested in the new inventions in Europe at the time. He travelled to Britain and to Holland, in secret, to learn about their way of life.

▲ Peter the Great studies shipbuilding in England

▲ Catherine the Great's sleigh

Peter wanted a strong navy for Russia, so he worked in shipyards to learn how ships were built. He took back scientists and engineers to modernize his country.

Peter's armies defeated Sweden, Persia and Turkey, and his empire grew bigger. He built the Baltic port of St Petersburg, which he called his 'window on the west'.

In 1762, Tsar Peter III was murdered. His wife, Catherine the Great, took over and ruled until 1796. Under Catherine's rule, the empire grew to include lands in the south and east.

The empire at war

In 1812, the French emperor, Napoleon, invaded Russia. Thousands of French soldiers died in the snow. Russia then fought France and Britain in the Crimean War, 1854-6. In 1904-5 they fought Japan.

The Russians had to pay for the wars, but they had no say in running their country.

After a rebellion in 1905, Tsar Nicolas II set up a Parliament. However, it did not have much power. When Russia went to war against Germany in 1914, another revolution was close.

▼ Soup for hungry families

Red, white and blue

Russian armies fought against Germany in the First World War. By 1917 they needed food and weapons. There were strikes and protests.

In October 1917, revolution came to Russia. The rebels were led by V.I. Lenin, and were called Bolsheviks. They flew the red flag over Moscow, so people called them the 'Reds'. Those Russians who fought them were called the 'Whites'. The country became the Union of Soviet Socialist Republics (USSR), or the Soviet Union.

▲ Red Guards light a fire in Petrograd, October 1917

▲ A Soviet soldier meets an American soldier, 1945

Lenin died in 1924. The new leader, Joseph Stalin, ruled by terror. People who did not agree with him were killed or imprisoned. Everyone was afraid of the secret police. Poor workers starved.

The Second World War

In this war, the Soviet Union joined France, Britain and the USA against Germany. More than 20 million Russians died. The brave people of Stalingrad (now Volgograd) helped to win the war. In 1945 the Red Army, with the Allies, invaded Germany, and the war ended.

Towards a new Russia

After the Second World War, western countries such as the United States did not trust the USSR. This distrust was called the 'Cold War'. Both sides had nuclear weapons, but they did not use them.

In 1985 Mikhail Gorbachev became leader in the USSR. He wanted to end the 'Cold War', and he met other world leaders to talk about his ideas. This open talking was called *glasnost*.

In 1991 a new President, Boris Yeltsin, was elected. In 1992 the west welcomed the end of the Soviet Union. The new red, white and blue flag of the Russian Federation now flies over the Kremlin.

▼ These Russian dolls look like Russian political leaders!

Fact file

Flags

The red, white and blue flag of the Russian Federation was first used in the time of Peter the Great. The two-headed eagle is also a sign, or emblem, of Russia. The old Soviet Union's emblem was the workers' hammer and sickle. It stood for factories and farms.

National anthem

In 1993 President Yeltsin held a competition for words for a new song, or anthem. The music was written 100 years ago.

Government

Russia's Parliament is called the Federal Assembly. It has two parts, or Houses. The Council has 178 seats. The Duma has 450 seats. Half of the Duma's members are elected to represent areas of the country. The other half are elected from the political parties.

Religion

Most Christians belong to the Russian Orthodox Church. Others are Protestants or Roman Catholics. There are Buddhist temples and Islamic mosques. People who do not believe in God are called atheists.

Money

There are notes and coins for Russian *roubles*. The new banknotes for 100 and 500 *roubles* show the Russian flag.

Education

All children go to school from the ages of 6 to 16. They may go on to college or university. Education is free in Russia.

Newspapers and television

Russian popular newspapers are *Pravda* ('Truth'), and *Today*. One TV channel covers all Russia and the other five are local channels.

Some famous people

Alexander Nevsky (1220-63) was a warrior prince.

Catherine the Great (1729-96) ruled Russia for 34 years.

Leo Tolstoy (1828-1910) was a thinker and a writer.

Sofia Kovalevskaya (1850-91) was a mathematician.

Vladimir Ilyich Lenin (1870-1924) was a revolutionary.

Anna Pavlova (1885-1931) was a world-famous ballerina.

Sergei Eisenstein (1898-1948) made films about Russian history.

Dmitri Shostakovich (1906-75) was a famous musician.

Alexander Solzhenitsyn (1918-) wrote about Stalin's prison camps.

Yuri Gagarin (1934-68) was the first man in space.

Valentina Tereshkova (1937-) was the first woman in space.

Olga Korbut (1955-) a gymnast who has won 3 Olympic medals.

Some key events in history

c.**440**BC Attila the Hun attacked from the east.

AD**988** Vladimir, The Grand Duke of Kiev, became a Christian.

1237-38 the Tartars invaded and Kiev fell.

1480 Moscow ruled Russia.

1713 St Petersburg became the new capital of Russia.

1812 Napoleon's army retreated from Moscow.

1905 Revolution. The *tsar* agreed to hold elections.

1917 The Bolshevik revolution.

1918 The last *tsar* and his family were shot.

1942-3 Stalingrad held out against the Germans.

1985 Mikhail Gorbachev was elected leader of the Communist Party.

1990 The Communists voted to end one-party rule.

1991 Gorbachev resigned. Boris Yeltsin elected President.

Index